Copyright © 2024
No part of this publication may be reproduced in any way without the author's permission, except when quoted and referenced with a full and correct citation.

This book is dedicated to my entire family—those who came before me, those who are with me now, and those who will come after me.

TABLE OF CONTENTS

- Introduction 5
  - Welcome to the World of AI 5
  - Why AI Matters for Teens 5
- Chapter 1: Understanding Artificial Intelligence 6
  - What is Artificial Intelligence? 6
  - History of AI 6
  - Types of AI: Narrow vs. General 6
- Chapter 2: How AI Works 9
  - Machine Learning Basics 9
  - Neural Networks and Deep Learning 9
  - Training and Testing Models 9
  - Common Algorithms Used in AI 10
- Chapter 3: Real-World Applications of AI 13
  - AI in Entertainment and Gaming 13
  - AI in Healthcare 13
  - AI in Education 13
  - AI in Social Media and Personalization 13
- Chapter 4: Ethical Considerations in AI 15
  - Bias and Fairness in AI 15
  - Privacy Concerns 15
  - Job Automation and Economic Impact 15
  - AI and Social Responsibility 16
- Chapter 5: Getting Started with AI Projects 18
  - Tools and Resources for Learning AI 18
  - Programming Languages for AI Development 18
  - DIY AI Projects for Teens 18
  - Online Courses and Communities 19
  - Chapter 6: Future Trends and Opportunities in AI 21
  - Emerging Technologies in AI 21
  - Careers in AI for Teens 21
  - How AI Will Shape the Future 22
- Conclusion 24
- Further Readings and Technical Resources 25

Introduction

Welcome to the World of AI

Welcome to the fascinating world of Artificial Intelligence (AI)! In this introductory chapter, we'll embark on a journey to explore the fundamental concepts of AI, understand its significance in today's world, and discover what lies ahead in this rapidly evolving field.

Why AI Matters for Teens

As the ever-evolving technology landscape changes in front of our eyes, there have been advancements in the field of Artificial Intelligence that cannot go unnoticed. Everything from Generative AI, ChatGPT and Large Language Models or LLMs. These advancements have the ability to impact our lives young and old in ways we could not have imagined just 10 or 20 years ago. These advancements are more than just apps for amusement, TikTok anyone? They will advance with us and drive new ideas and innovations to arise. Including content in this book. Yes you read right, some of the content in this book has been derived by Artificial Intelligence. Who said AI can't be helpful? ●It will become imperative to understand how in its essence AI functions and its real applications in our daily lives.

Be sure to be on the lookout for our image prompt after each chapter that can be used to depict some of the AI images used after almost all chapters. Type them into your favorite AI Image Generator like Midjourney of Microsoft Copilot. Happy Prompting!!

Now let's dive into Artificial Intelligence and understand its significance in today's world, and discover what lies ahead in this rapidly evolving field.

Chapter 1: Understanding Artificial Intelligence

Welcome to Chapter 1 of our Beginner's Guide to AI for Teens! In this chapter, we'll dive deeper into the concept of Artificial Intelligence (AI) and lay the foundation for our exploration of this fascinating field. By the end of this chapter, you'll have a solid understanding of what AI is, its historical evolution, and its various applications in our everyday lives.

What is Artificial Intelligence?

Artificial Intelligence, often abbreviated as AI, refers to the development of computer systems capable of performing tasks that typically require human intelligence. These tasks may include learning from data, recognizing patterns, making decisions, understanding natural language, and even engaging in creative endeavors. AI seeks to replicate and emulate human cognitive abilities in machines, enabling them to automate complex processes, solve problems, and adapt to new situations.

History of AI

The history of AI dates back to ancient times, with myths and legends recounting tales of artificial beings crafted by humans. However, the modern era of AI began in the mid-20th century with the pioneering work of scientists and researchers who sought to create intelligent machines. One of the seminal moments in AI history was the invention of the digital computer, which laid the groundwork for computational approaches to intelligence. Over the decades, AI has witnessed significant advancements, driven by breakthroughs in algorithms, hardware, and data availability.

Types of AI: Narrow vs. General

AI can be classified into two main categories: Narrow AI (Weak AI) and General AI (Strong AI). Narrow AI refers to systems designed to perform specific tasks or solve particular problems within a limited domain. Examples of narrow AI applications include virtual assistants like Siri, recommendation algorithms on e-commerce platforms, and facial recognition systems. In contrast, General AI aims to replicate the breadth and flexibility of human intelligence, exhibiting proficiency across a wide range of cognitive tasks. While General AI remains a long-term goal of AI research, most current AI systems are narrow in scope, focusing on specific tasks or domains.

Examples of AI in Everyday Life

AI has become increasingly integrated into various aspects of our daily lives, enriching our experiences and enhancing efficiency. From personalized recommendations on streaming platforms to predictive text suggestions on smartphones, AI technologies are ubiquitous and omnipresent. AI-powered applications and services are revolutionizing industries such as healthcare, finance, transportation, and entertainment, driving innovation and reshaping the way we interact with technology.

Image depicting the concept of artificial intelligence: Prompt: "Generate an image of a futuristic robot with human-like features and advanced technological elements, symbolizing the concept of artificial intelligence."

Chapter 2: How AI Works

Welcome to Chapter 2 of our Beginner's Guide to AI for Teens! In this chapter, we'll delve into the inner workings of Artificial Intelligence (AI) and explore the fundamental principles that enable machines to exhibit intelligent behavior. By the end of this chapter, you'll have a deeper understanding of how AI systems learn, reason, and make decisions.

Machine Learning Basics

At the heart of many AI systems lies the concept of Machine Learning (ML), a subfield of AI focused on developing algorithms that allow computers to learn from data. In traditional programming, humans explicitly instruct computers on how to perform tasks through predefined rules and instructions. In contrast, in machine learning, computers learn to perform tasks by analyzing data and identifying patterns or relationships within that data. This process of learning from data enables AI systems to improve their performance over time without being explicitly programmed for each specific task.

Neural Networks and Deep Learning

Neural Networks are a class of machine learning algorithms inspired by the structure and function of the human brain. These networks consist of interconnected nodes, or neurons, organized into layers. Each neuron receives input signals, processes them, and generates an output signal, which serves as input to subsequent layers. Deep Learning, a subset of machine learning, refers to the training of neural networks with multiple layers (hence the term "deep"), allowing them to learn increasingly complex representations of data. Deep learning has revolutionized AI by enabling remarkable advancements in areas such as image recognition, natural language processing, and autonomous driving.

Training and Testing Models

In the machine learning pipeline, AI models are trained on labeled datasets, where the input data is paired with corresponding output labels. During the training process, the model learns to map input data to output labels by adjusting its internal parameters through iterative optimization algorithms. Once trained, the model is evaluated on a separate dataset, called the test set, or training data, to assess its performance and generalization ability. This process of training and testing ensures that AI models can accurately perform tasks on unseen data, thereby demonstrating their effectiveness and reliability. (See Training and Testing Model Image)

Common Algorithms Used in AI

AI encompasses a diverse range of algorithms and techniques tailored for different tasks and domains. Some common algorithms used in AI include:

- Linear Regression: Used for modeling the relationship between input variables and continuous output values.
- Logistic Regression: Used for binary classification tasks, where the output is a binary variable.
- Decision Trees: Used for classification and regression tasks by partitioning the input space into smaller regions.
- Support Vector Machines (SVM): Used for classification and regression tasks by finding the optimal hyperplane that separates different classes or predicts continuous values.

Flow diagram depicting the process of a simple AI Algorithm:

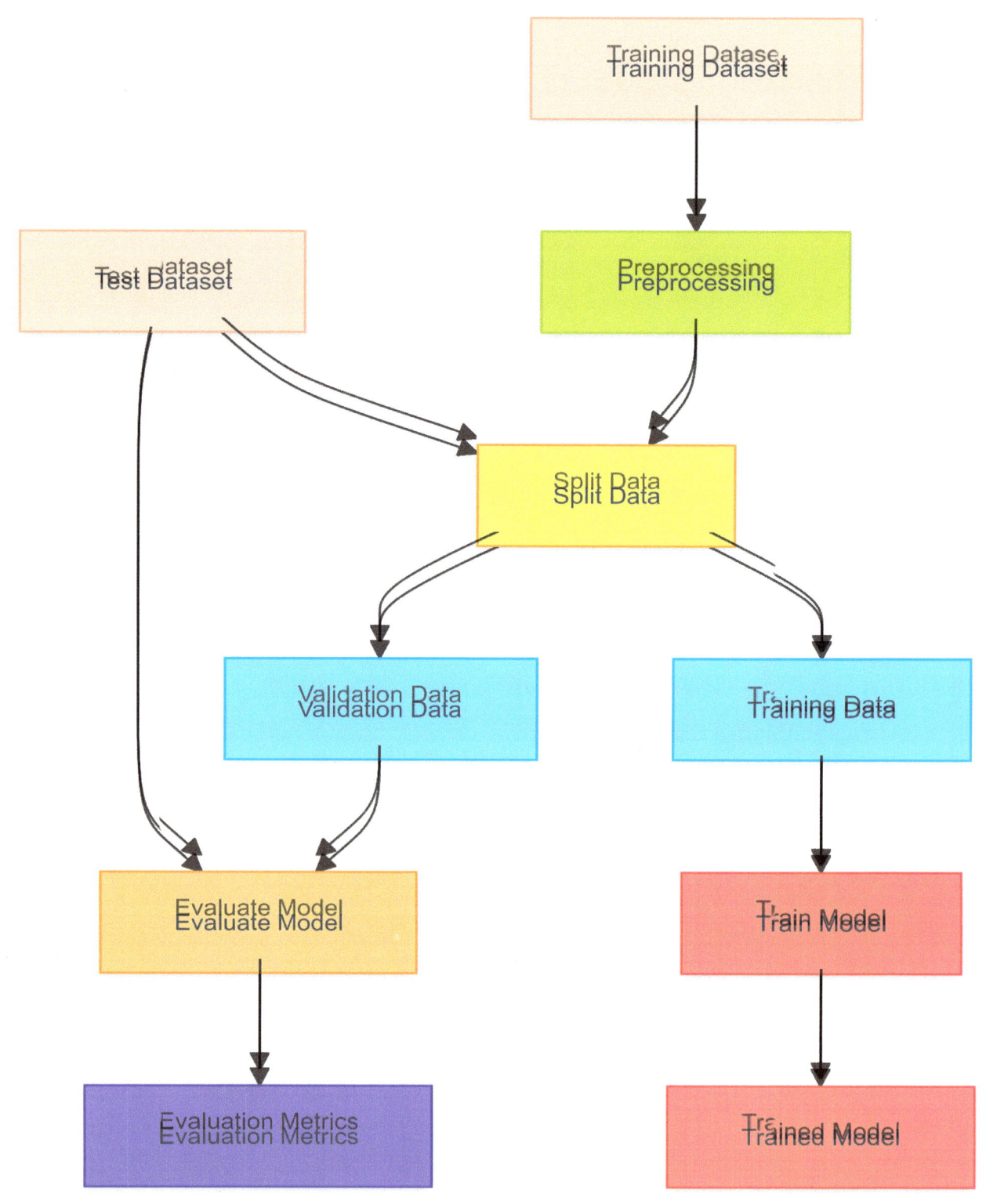

Below are steps that break down the flow diagram above into

manageable steps focusing on the implementation of a simple AI algorithm—training and testing a machine learning model.

Step 1: Define the Objective
Objective: Determine what problem you are solving with your AI model.

Step 2: Collect and Explore the Data
Objective: Gather the relevant data and perform exploratory data analysis (EDA) to understand its distribution, identify missing values, etc.

Step 3: Preprocess the Data
Objective: Clean and prepare the data for model training, including handling missing values, normalizing, or standardizing the data.

Step 4: Split the Data into Training and Test Sets
Objective: Split the dataset into a training set and a test set (and optionally a validation set).

Step 5: Choose a Model
Objective: Select an appropriate machine learning algorithm for your problem.

Step 6: Train the Model
Objective: Use the training dataset to train your machine learning model.

Step 7: Validate the Model
Objective: Use a validation set (if available) to tune hyperparameters and validate the model performance.

Step 8: Evaluate the Model on the Test Set
Objective: Use the test set to evaluate the performance of the trained model.

Step 9: Interpret and Communicate the Results
Objective: Analyze the evaluation metrics, interpret the results, and communicate your findings.

Chapter 3: Real-World Applications of AI

Welcome to Chapter 3 of our Beginner's Guide to AI for Teens! In this chapter, we'll explore the diverse and impactful ways in which Artificial Intelligence (AI) is applied in various industries and domains. From entertainment to healthcare, AI technologies are revolutionizing our world and shaping the future in unprecedented ways.

AI in Entertainment and Gaming

In the realm of entertainment and gaming, AI plays a crucial role in enhancing user experiences, enabling personalized recommendations, and creating immersive virtual worlds. Recommendation algorithms analyze user preferences and behavior to suggest movies, music, or video games tailored to individual tastes. AI-powered game engines utilize techniques such as procedural generation and reinforcement learning to dynamically adapt gameplay and create dynamic, challenging experiences for players.

AI in Healthcare

AI is transforming healthcare by enabling more accurate diagnostics, personalized treatment plans, and proactive disease prevention strategies. Medical imaging technologies, such as MRI and CT scans, leverage AI algorithms to analyze images and detect abnormalities or signs of disease. Natural language processing (NLP) algorithms are employed to extract insights from clinical notes, medical records, and research literature, facilitating data-driven decision-making and improving patient outcomes.

AI in Education

In the field of education, AI is revolutionizing teaching and learning methodologies, making education more accessible, adaptive, and personalized. Intelligent tutoring systems use AI algorithms to assess students' learning progress, identify areas of difficulty, and provide tailored feedback and support. Adaptive learning platforms dynamically adjust learning materials and activities based on students' individual strengths, weaknesses, and learning styles, optimizing the learning experience for each student.

AI in Social Media and Personalization

AI technologies power social media platforms, enabling content curation, user engagement analysis, and targeted advertising. Recommendation algorithms analyze users' browsing history, interactions, and preferences to suggest relevant content, products, or services. Natural language processing (NLP) algorithms are used to analyze user-generated content, detect sentiment, and identify emerging trends, enabling social media platforms to deliver personalized experiences and optimize user engagement.

Visual representation of a neural network architecture: Prompt: "Generate an abstract visual representation of a neural network architecture, with interconnected nodes and layers, illustrating how neural networks function in artificial intelligence."

Chapter 4: Ethical Considerations in AI

Welcome to Chapter 4 of our Beginner's Guide to AI for Teens! In this chapter, we'll explore the ethical implications of Artificial Intelligence (AI) and discuss the importance of responsible AI development and deployment. As AI technologies continue to advance and integrate into various aspects of our lives, it's crucial to consider the potential societal impacts and ethical dilemmas that arise.

Bias and Fairness in AI

One of the key ethical concerns in AI is the presence of bias in algorithms and data. AI systems learn from historical data, which may reflect societal biases and inequalities. As a result, AI algorithms may inadvertently perpetuate or amplify existing biases, leading to unfair treatment or discrimination against certain individuals or groups. It's essential for developers to mitigate bias in AI systems by carefully curating training data, designing transparent and accountable algorithms, and regularly monitoring and evaluating system performance for fairness and equity.

Privacy Concerns

AI technologies often rely on vast amounts of data to train and improve their performance. However, the collection, storage, and processing of personal data raise significant privacy concerns. AI systems may inadvertently compromise individuals' privacy by analyzing sensitive information without their consent or awareness. It's crucial for organizations and developers to implement robust privacy safeguards, such as data anonymization, encryption, and consent mechanisms, to protect individuals' privacy rights and mitigate the risk of unauthorized data access or misuse.

Job Automation and Economic Impact

The increasing automation of tasks and jobs by AI technologies raises concerns about unemployment, job displacement, and economic inequality. While AI has the potential to boost productivity, drive innovation, and create new job opportunities, it also poses challenges for workers whose jobs are susceptible to automation. It's essential for policymakers, businesses, and society as a whole to address these challenges through initiatives such as retraining programs, workforce development, and social safety nets to ensure that the benefits of AI are shared equitably and inclusively.

AI and Social Responsibility

As creators and consumers of AI technologies, we all have a responsibility to use AI in ways that benefit society and uphold ethical principles. This includes promoting transparency, accountability, and fairness in AI development and deployment, advocating for policies and regulations that safeguard individuals' rights and well-being, and actively engaging in discussions and debates about the ethical implications of AI. By fostering a culture of ethical awareness and responsibility, we can harness the potential of AI to create a more just, equitable, and inclusive future for all.

Examples of real-world applications of AI: Prompt: "Generate images depicting various real-world applications of artificial intelligence, such as self-driving cars navigating city streets, virtual assistants interacting with users, and smart devices enhancing daily life."

Chapter 5: Getting Started with AI Projects

Welcome to Chapter 5 of our Beginner's Guide to AI for Teens! In this chapter, we'll dive into practical strategies and resources for embarking on your own AI projects. Whether you're a beginner or have some experience with programming and machine learning, there are plenty of opportunities to explore and experiment with AI. Let's get started!

Tools and Resources for Learning AI

There are numerous tools and resources available to help you learn about AI and develop your skills. Online platforms such as Coursera, Udacity, and edX offer courses on topics ranging from machine learning and deep learning to computer vision and natural language processing. Additionally, websites like Kaggle and GitHub provide access to datasets, tutorials, and code repositories for AI projects. Take advantage of these resources to explore different concepts, algorithms, and applications of AI at your own pace.

Programming Languages for AI Development

Python is the most popular programming language for AI development, thanks to its simplicity, versatility, and rich ecosystem of libraries and frameworks. Libraries such as TensorFlow, PyTorch, and scikit-learn provide powerful tools for building and training AI models, while libraries like OpenCV and NLTK offer capabilities for computer vision and natural language processing tasks. Familiarize yourself with Python and these libraries to start experimenting with AI projects and exploring real-world applications.

DIY AI Projects for Teens

Here are some beginner-friendly AI projects to get you started:

1. **Image Classification:** Build a model that can classify images into different categories, such as cats vs. dogs or handwritten digits.
2. **Sentiment Analysis:** Develop a sentiment analysis tool that can analyze text data and determine the sentiment (positive, negative, or neutral) of a given piece of text.
3. **Voice Recognition:** Create a voice recognition system that can recognize spoken commands or transcribe speech into text.
4. **Chatbot:** Design a chatbot that can engage in conversation with users and provide responses based on predefined rules or machine learning algorithms.
5. **Gesture Recognition:** Build a system that can recognize hand gestures captured by a webcam and perform actions based on the detected gestures.

Online Courses and Communities

Joining online communities and participating in forums and discussion groups can be invaluable for learning, sharing knowledge, and seeking support from fellow AI enthusiasts. Websites like Stack Overflow, Reddit (e.g., r/MachineLearning), and AI-specific forums offer platforms for asking questions, sharing insights, and collaborating on projects. Additionally, participating in online courses and workshops can provide structured learning experiences and opportunities to connect with experts and peers in the field.

Examples of code snippets or programming interfaces used in AI development:
Prompt: "Generate images of code snippets or programming interfaces commonly used in artificial intelligence development, showcasing syntax highlighting, function definitions, and variable assignments."

Chapter 6: Future Trends and Opportunities in AI

Welcome to Chapter 6 of our Beginner's Guide to AI for Teens! In this chapter, we'll peer into the future of Artificial Intelligence (AI) and explore emerging trends, technologies, and opportunities that are shaping the landscape of AI research and applications. As AI continues to advance at a rapid pace, there are endless possibilities for innovation, exploration, and impact.

Emerging Technologies in AI

Several emerging technologies hold promise for advancing the field of AI and unlocking new capabilities:

- Reinforcement Learning: A type of machine learning where agents learn to interact with an environment to achieve specific goals through trial and error. Reinforcement learning has shown remarkable success in domains such as robotics, autonomous vehicles, and game playing.
- Generative Adversarial Networks (GANs): A class of deep learning models that can generate realistic and high-quality synthetic data, such as images, audio, and text. GANs have applications in image synthesis, data augmentation, and creative arts.
- Quantum Computing: Quantum computing has the potential to revolutionize AI by enabling faster computation and more efficient algorithms for tasks such as optimization, simulation, and machine learning. While still in its infancy, quantum computing holds promise for tackling complex AI challenges that are currently intractable with classical computers.

Careers in AI for Teens

As AI technologies continue to evolve and proliferate, there are abundant career opportunities for teens interested in pursuing a career in AI:

- Machine Learning Engineer: Develop and deploy machine learning models for various applications, such as image recognition, natural language processing, and recommendation systems.
- Data Scientist: Analyze and interpret large datasets to extract insights and inform decision-making using statistical techniques and machine learning algorithms.
- AI Researcher: Conduct research to advance the state-of-the-art in AI, develop new algorithms and methodologies, and publish findings in academic journals and conferences.
- AI Ethics Consultant: Advise organizations on ethical considerations and implications of AI technologies, design and implement responsible AI policies and guidelines, and advocate for fairness, transparency, and accountability in AI development and deployment.

How AI Will Shape the Future

AI is poised to have a profound impact on nearly every aspect of our lives, transforming industries, reshaping economies, and redefining human-machine interactions:

- Healthcare: AI technologies will revolutionize healthcare by enabling more accurate diagnostics, personalized treatment plans, and proactive disease prevention strategies.
- Transportation: AI-powered autonomous vehicles will reshape the transportation industry, improving safety, efficiency, and accessibility while reducing congestion and emissions.

- Education: AI will transform education by personalizing learning experiences, automating administrative tasks, and providing adaptive tutoring and feedback to students.
- Environmental Sustainability: AI can play a critical role in addressing global challenges such as climate change, resource conservation, and environmental monitoring through data-driven insights and optimize

Visual representations of potential career paths and opportunities in AI for teens: Prompt: "Create visual representations of potential career paths and opportunities in artificial intelligence for teens, showcasing diverse roles and specialties within the field, such as machine learning engineer, data scientist, and AI researcher."

Conclusion

Congratulations on completing our Beginner's Guide to AI for Teens! Throughout this book, we've embarked on an exciting journey into the world of Artificial Intelligence, exploring fundamental concepts, real-world applications, ethical considerations, and future trends in this rapidly evolving field.

As you reflect on your journey, remember that AI is more than just a technological innovation—it's a tool for creativity, innovation, and empowerment. Whether you're interested in coding, problem-solving, or making a positive impact on the world, AI offers countless opportunities for exploration and discovery.

As you continue to explore the world of AI, remember to stay curious, open-minded, and adaptable. The field of AI is vast and ever-changing, with endless possibilities for learning and growth. Whether you're pursuing a career in AI, developing your own AI projects, or simply staying informed about the latest advancements, your journey in AI is just beginning.

Thank you for joining us on this journey, and we wish you the best of luck in all your future endeavors in the exciting world of Artificial Intelligence!

Keep exploring, keep innovating, and keep dreaming big!

P.S. Reminder, some content here in this book was created using AI with some help from a human. Not bad for a machine!

Further Readings and Technical Resources

By exploring these resources, you'll deepen your understanding of Artificial Intelligence, build practical skills, and stay up-to-date with the latest developments in the field. Happy learning!

Books:

1. "Artificial Intelligence: A Guide for Thinking Humans" by Melanie Mitchell
   - A comprehensive introduction to AI, explaining complex concepts in a relatable and understandable way.
2. "Python Machine Learning" by Sebastian Raschka and Vahid Mirjalili
   - Perfect for beginners, this book provides a hands-on approach to learning machine learning with Python.
3. "The Hundred-Page Machine Learning Book" by Andriy Burkov
   - A concise and straightforward introduction to machine learning, covering essential concepts and techniques.
4. "AI Superpowers: China, Silicon Valley, and the New World Order" by Kai-Fu Lee
   - A fascinating look at the global impact of AI, comparing the advancements and strategies of China and the United States.
5. "You Look Like a Thing and I Love You: How AI Works and Why It's Making the World a Weirder Place" by Janelle Shane
   - A humorous and accessible exploration of AI, providing insight into how AI algorithms work and their often unexpected outcomes.

Online Courses:

1. [Coursera: Introduction to Artificial Intelligence (AI)](#)
   - A beginner-friendly course offered by Coursera and taught by AI expert Andrew Ng. It covers the basics of AI, its applications, and its future.

2. [edX: CS50's Introduction to Artificial Intelligence with Python](#)
    - Offered by Harvard University, this course provides an in-depth introduction to AI, focusing on concepts like search algorithms, classification, and neural networks.
3. [Udacity: Intro to Machine Learning with PyTorch](#)
    - This course offers practical skills in machine learning using Python and PyTorch, ideal for students ready to start building their own AI models.
4. [Khan Academy: Introduction to Algorithms](#)
    - A great resource for understanding the algorithms that power AI systems, presented in an easy-to-follow format.

Websites & Communities:

1. [Kaggle](#)
    - A platform where you can practice your AI and machine learning skills by working on real-world datasets and participating in competitions.
2. [Towards Data Science](#)
    - A popular blog on Medium that features articles on AI, machine learning, and data science, written by experts and practitioners in the field.
3. [AI4ALL](#)
    - A nonprofit organization focused on increasing diversity and inclusion in AI education. They offer programs, resources, and community support for students interested in AI.
4. [Fast.ai](#)
    - An online resource offering free courses, tutorials, and community forums for those interested in deep learning and AI, with a focus on practical implementation.

Tools & Libraries:

1. [TensorFlow](#)

- An open-source machine learning library developed by Google, widely used for building and training AI models.
2. [PyTorch](#)
    - Another popular open-source machine learning library, known for its flexibility and ease of use, particularly in research and development.
3. [Scikit-Learn](#)
    - A powerful library for machine learning in Python, offering simple and efficient tools for data analysis and modeling.
4. [Google Colab](#)
    - A free, cloud-based platform that allows you to write and execute Python code, making it easy to experiment with AI and machine learning projects.

Podcasts & Videos:

1. [The AI Alignment Podcast](#)
    - A podcast exploring the technical and philosophical challenges of creating safe and beneficial AI.
2. [Data Skeptic](#)
    - A podcast that covers a wide range of topics in data science, machine learning, and AI, aimed at both beginners and experts.
3. [YouTube: 3Blue1Brown's Neural Networks Playlist](#)
    - A visually engaging series that explains how neural networks work, using intuitive graphics and step-by-step tutorials.

Appendix: Glossary of AI Terms

This glossary provides definitions and explanations of key terms and concepts in Artificial Intelligence, helping readers navigate the terminology and deepen their understanding of the field.

Artificial Intelligence (AI): The simulation of human intelligence processes by machines, including learning, reasoning, problem-solving, perception, and language understanding.

Machine Learning (ML): A subset of AI that focuses on developing algorithms and techniques that enable computers to learn from data and improve their performance over time without being explicitly programmed.

Deep Learning: A subset of machine learning that employs artificial neural networks with multiple layers (hence the term "deep") to learn complex representations of data.

Neural Networks: Computing systems inspired by the biological neural networks of the human brain, consisting of interconnected nodes (neurons) organized into layers.

Data Science: The interdisciplinary field that combines techniques from statistics, computer science, and domain expertise to extract insights and knowledge from large datasets.

Algorithm: A set of step-by-step instructions or rules for solving a particular problem or performing a specific task.

Model: A mathematical representation or abstraction of a real-world system or phenomenon, used in machine learning to make predictions or decisions based on input data.

Training Data: Labeled dataset used to train machine learning models by providing input data paired with corresponding output labels.

Test Data: Separate dataset used to evaluate the performance of machine learning models after training, ensuring that the models can generalize to unseen data.

Bias: Systematic error or distortion in AI algorithms or data that leads to unfair treatment or discrimination against certain individuals or groups.

Fairness: The principle of treating all individuals or groups impartially and without bias in AI systems, ensuring equitable outcomes for all.

Privacy: The protection of individuals' personal data and information from unauthorized access, use, or disclosure.

Job Automation: The process of replacing human labor with AI and automation technologies to perform tasks and jobs more efficiently and cost-effectively.

Ethics: The moral principles and values that govern the behavior and decisions of individuals and organizations, including considerations of right and wrong in AI development and deployment.

Transparency: The principle of openness and clarity in AI systems, ensuring that their operation, decision-making processes, and outcomes are understandable and explainable.

Accountability: The principle of holding individuals and organizations responsible for the consequences of their actions and decisions in AI development and deployment.

Reinforcement Learning: A type of machine learning where agents learn to interact with an environment to achieve specific goals through trial and error.

Generative Adversarial Networks (GANs): A class of deep learning models that can generate realistic and high-quality synthetic data, such as images, audio, and text.

Quantum Computing: A computing paradigm that utilizes the principles of quantum mechanics to perform computation, offering the potential for faster and more efficient algorithms for AI tasks.